Who Was
Charles Darwin?

Who Was
Charles Darwin?

by Deborah Hopkinson

illustrated by Nancy Harrison

Penguin Workshop

For my wonderful and curious son, Dimitri, who loves
to ask questions—just like Charles Darwin—DH

To my sisters, for their unwavering belief that anything is
possible and always cheering me on—NH

Acknowledgment

Special thanks to Delbert Hutchison,
Assistant Professor of Biology, Whitman College, for sharing
his enthusiasm about Charles Darwin and making helpful
suggestions on the manuscript. Any errors are my own.

PENGUIN WORKSHOP
An Imprint of Penguin Random House LLC, New York

ISBN 9780448437644

40 39 38

Contents

Who Was
Charles Darwin?

 Charles Darwin took a five-year trip around the world on a ship called the *Beagle*, but he liked staying home best of all. He lived in a small English village where he raised pigeons, played with his children, and puttered in his garden.

Although he lived a quiet life, Charles Darwin started a revolution—a revolution of thought.

People have always wondered how life on Earth began. When Charles Darwin lived, most people in Europe and America believed God created the entire world in six days, just as it says in the Bible. But Charles Darwin was not most people. The *Beagle* voyage taught him to be a true scientist—to look closely at nature, question everything, and think in a new way about how life on Earth started. He showed how living things could naturally change, or evolve, over a long period of time.

Was Charles Darwin a genius? He didn't think so. Charles thought of himself as simply a scientist. And like all good scientists, Charles was curious—so curious he was never afraid to ask hard questions—and he looked for answers based on what he saw.

Charles Darwin knew his ideas would shock people. They did. Yet today scientists accept evolution as a fact. Charles Darwin is as important as ever.

Charles Darwin changed history. How did he do it?

Chapter 1
An Ordinary Boy

Charles Robert Darwin was born on February 12, 1809, in Shrewsbury, a small village in England. His family was well-off. His father was a respected, successful doctor. His mother, Susanna, was a daughter of Josiah Wedgwood, who owned a famous china factory.

The Darwins lived in a large house called "The Mount." It was near the River Severn.

Charles loved his home. Even as a boy he was curious about nature. He spent hours in the family garden. Once, his father asked Charles to count the peony blossoms in the garden.

Charles counted 384 flowers! Already Charles was learning to look carefully at nature.

Charles liked climbing trees, watching birds, and taking walks. He played and fished on the banks of the river. Best of all, Charles loved collecting. He collected stones, pebbles, and bird eggs. (He made sure to take only one egg from each nest.) When he wasn't exploring or collecting, Charles curled up with a book.

Charles's mother died in 1817, when he was only eight. His three older sisters and older brother stepped in to help care for Charles and his little sister, Catherine.

During this time in England, many boys were sent to live at school. When Charles was nine, his father sent him to nearby Shrewsbury School. Charles hated it. He didn't like sleeping in the crowded dormitory. He wasn't good at memorizing. Whenever Charles had to learn a poem, he'd forget it two days later.

Charles also missed home. He was very close with his older brother Erasmus. He was glad his school was only a mile away. Sometimes in the evening Charles would sneak out.

Charles would race home to see his family and Spark, his dog. Then he had to run fast to get back before the school doors closed for the night. Luckily, he was a fast runner!

At home, Charles and Erasmus had their own chemistry lab. The lab was in a tool shed in the garden. Charles loved doing experiments so much, his friends called him "Gas."

One day, Charles's teacher found out about the lab. He said Charles was wasting his time. He called the experiments "useless." How wrong this teacher was!

Charles's father hoped both his sons would find good, respectable professions. He wanted them to become doctors, like him.

Erasmus was sent to medical school in Edinburgh, Scotland. And since Charles hated Shrewsbury School so much, Dr. Darwin let Charles go too. He hoped that Charles would make something of himself in Scotland.

EDINBURGH

In 1825, at age sixteen, Charles began taking classes at Edinburgh University. After watching two operations, Charles knew medicine wasn't for him. But, partly to please his father, Charles kept going to classes.

SURGERY IN CHARLES DARWIN'S TIME

"I saw two very bad operations, one on a child, but I rushed away before they were completed . . . The two cases fairly haunted me for many a long year."
—Charles Darwin

IN THE MID-1820S, WHEN CHARLES WAS IN MEDICAL SCHOOL, OPERATIONS WERE STILL PERFORMED WITHOUT ANESTHESIA, OR PAINKILLERS. FOR CENTURIES, DOCTORS HAD SEARCHED TO FIND WAYS TO DEADEN THE PAIN OF SURGERY. THEY TRIED ALCOHOL AND SUBSTANCES FROM PLANTS, SUCH AS OPIUM FROM POPPIES. SOMETIMES THEY HIT PATIENTS TO KNOCK THEM UNCONSCIOUS. BUT NOTHING REALLY WORKED. THEN IN 1844, HORACE WELLS, AN AMERICAN DENTIST, DISCOVERED THAT NITROUS OXIDE COULD HELP PREVENT PAIN WHEN SOMEONE'S TOOTH WAS PULLED. AND IN 1846, IN BOSTON, A PATIENT WAS GIVEN SULFURIC ETHER, A GAS, DURING SURGERY. THE SURGEON REMOVED A TUMOR FROM THE MAN'S JAW AND THE MAN DIDN'T FEEL ANY PAIN! A NEW WORLD OF MEDICINE HAD BEGUN.

When Charles went home for the summer, he didn't dare tell his father how he felt about medicine. Instead, he spent all his time hunting and riding. Finally, after his second year of medical school, Charles confessed that he didn't want to be a doctor. His father was angry. He worried that Charles would never amount to anything.

What next? Charles had to have *some* profession, so Dr. Darwin sent him to Cambridge

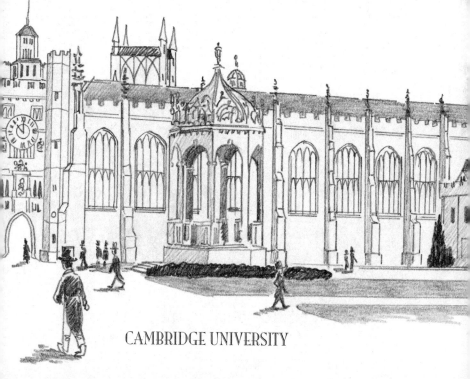

CAMBRIDGE UNIVERSITY

University. Charles would study to be a minister in the Church of England. Being a minister was a respectable career. And since many ministers at that time studied nature, it seemed a good choice for Charles.

Charles still enjoyed science and nature best of all. His favorite hobby was collecting beetles. Years later, Charles recalled a funny story about his beetles. One day he saw two rare beetles and grabbed one in each hand. Then he spotted a third new kind. He couldn't bear to lose it.

So Charles popped the one in his right hand into his mouth. Suddenly it shot out some bitter fluid. Yuck! It stung so much that Charles spit it out as fast as he could. He dropped the third beetle, too. After all that, he ended up with only one beetle.

Charles's favorite professor at Cambridge was John Stevens Henslow. Professor Henslow taught botany, the study of plants. The two became friends and often took walks together. This friendship would change Charles's life.

Chapter 2
Chance of a Lifetime

Charles graduated from college in the summer of 1831 at age twenty-two. He planned to return to Cambridge in the fall to do extra work, then become a minister. In the Church of England, ministers can marry and have a family. Charles would be in charge of a country church, preach sermons, and help people. In his free time, he'd be able to explore nature.

In August, Charles got a letter from his friend Professor Henslow. The professor had a surprising question for him. Would Charles like to travel around the world?

A captain in the British navy named Robert FitzRoy

would soon sail around the world. His ship, the HMS *Beagle*, would be gone for at least two years.

There were several reasons for the trip. Great Britain wanted to do more trading with countries in South America. The captain and his crew would make maps of the ocean waters around

ROBERT FITZROY

South America so other ships would know the best routes to take.

Captain FitzRoy liked science and nature. He wanted to bring along a naturalist, someone who studies nature. The naturalist would have to pay his own way. But he'd be able to collect plants and animals. Captain FitzRoy also wanted someone to talk to and share meals with on the voyage. (It wasn't proper for the captain to be friends with the sailors under his command.)

Professor Henslow knew Charles loved nature. And Charles had a pleasant, friendly manner. He'd make a good companion for the captain on the long, lonely trip.

Charles rushed to ask his father's permission. At first Dr. Darwin didn't approve. What about the danger? What about Charles's plan to become a minister? Wasn't he ever going to settle down? It all sounded like a "wild scheme."

Charles's heart sank. Traveling on the *Beagle* seemed much more exciting than being a minister. And although sea voyages could be dangerous,

Charles didn't think his father needed to worry.

Luckily, Charles's uncle, Josiah Wedgwood, helped persuade Dr. Darwin to say yes. Charles packed his things and said good-bye to his family. In October of 1831, he went to Plymouth, England.

Circumnavigation (going around the world on a ship) was fairly common by Charles's day. Three hundred years had passed since Ferdinand Magellan first circled the globe in 1522.

For the *Beagle*, however, there were many delays. First the ship had to be repaired. Then the weather

turned bad. Charles could do nothing but wait. To help pass time, he began to keep a diary. Charles decided to keep a journal of his entire voyage.

At last, on December 27, 1831, the *Beagle* set sail.

The *Beagle* was ninety feet and four inches long. Seventy-four people lived on board, including ten officers and thirty-eight seamen. The boat carried drinking water and food, including about six thousand tins of preserved meat. There were no refrigerators then.

"Not one inch of room is lost," Charles wrote.

Charles had to share a small room, called a "poop cabin," with two officers. His sleeping hammock was strung up over a table. During the day, the officers used the table to work on their maps and charts. Charles shared this same space.

On his first try, Charles couldn't even climb into his hammock. It kept swinging away from him. Finally he got in. But to stretch out his feet,

he had to take out one of the drawers built into the wall. It was a tight fit!

As it turned out, Charles spent a lot of time in his hammock. By the second day at sea, he got seasick. Charles suffered terribly during most of the trip. Charles once told a friend, "I hate every wave of the ocean."

The *Beagle's* first stop was the Cape Verde Islands. These tropical islands lie north of the equator, about five hundred miles off the western coast of Africa. The *Beagle* had been at sea for only about two weeks. But already Charles felt as if he'd stepped into another world.

Everything was new and different. Charles saw coconut and orange trees. He walked on volcanic rocks. Right away he started collecting new insects, new flowers, and new sea creatures.

Charles also became curious about how the island had been formed. Before leaving England, Captain FitzRoy had given Charles a new book called

SPAIN

CANARY ISLANDS

AFRICA

CAPE VERDE ISLANDS

Principles of Geology by Charles Lyell, a geologist. (Geologists study the history and structure of the Earth.)

At the time, people believed that God had created mountains, continents, and oceans in the same way God had created living things. But Lyell said something different. He proposed that the Earth had been formed over a long period of time, through natural processes, such as volcanoes and earthquakes.

Charles was fascinated by Lyell's bold thinking. Now, sitting on the island beach in the hot sun,

Charles had a wonderful idea. He would observe all the plants and animals and places he saw on his trip. He'd collect specimens, explore, and ask questions.

Perhaps he could write a book, too. Maybe he could discover new ways to look at the world.

Charles was filled with excitement. His life now had purpose. He would follow his heart and become a scientist.

Chapter 3
Charles Becomes a Scientist

Charles had lots of time to learn to think like a scientist. The *Beagle* voyage was supposed to last two years. Instead, it lasted five. During those years, Charles was at sea for only eighteen months. The rest of the time, he explored or hunted. When Charles was on land, the *Beagle* would usually be sailing nearby, charting the ocean waters.

In South America, Charles made seven long trips, traveling hundreds of miles on horseback. He also made dozens of shorter trips, including hunting trips. Since he

was a good shot, he often brought back fresh meat for the crew.

Whenever Charles explored, he scribbled notes in a small notebook. Back on the *Beagle*, he used his notes to make longer entries into his diary. He also worked on his plant and animal collections. He examined small creatures under a microscope.

He dried and preserved specimens. He cleaned and numbered bones. The sailors made wooden barrels, boxes, and crates for all his specimens.

Charles learned from Captain FitzRoy and the other officers. He noticed how carefully they kept their logbooks. Charles tried to keep detailed records, too. This helped him become a better scientist. In any experiment, a scientist must pay attention to every detail.

To catch sea creatures and tiny marine plants, Charles made his own net. He trawled it behind the ship. Charles was proud of his invention and made a sketch of it in his diary. When he wasn't too seasick, he sometimes helped catch fish for dinner.

Charles made his first major discovery in September 1832, nine months into the voyage. One day, he and Captain FitzRoy were in a small boat exploring the coast of Argentina. Charles caught sight of something that looked like a pile of bones, almost hidden by clay and soft rock. Charles wondered: could these be fossils?

The next day, Charles went back with his pickax and dug for hours. He found fossil skeletons from at least three large animals. One had an enormous head.

Charles had never seen any creature with big bones like these. Yet the skeletons reminded him of the smaller, live armadillos he'd seen nearby—and even eaten for dinner. Did the fossils belong to a creature related to living armadillos?

It was hard work to load the large fossil bones onto the *Beagle*. The sailors had to use pulleys and ropes. By the end, Charles was tired but pleased. He suspected that the bones belonged to creatures that had died off, or become extinct, long ago.

Charles didn't know exactly how or why creatures became extinct. But these fossils held important clues. Eventually, they would help him understand how populations, or groups, of animals change over time.

FOSSILS

A FOSSIL IS EITHER A PRESERVED PIECE OR AN IMPRESSION OF AN ANIMAL OR PLANT THAT DIED LONG AGO. FOSSILS ARE PRESERVED IN THE EARTH'S CRUST. THE WORD *FOSSIL* COMES FROM A LATIN WORD MEANING "TO DIG."

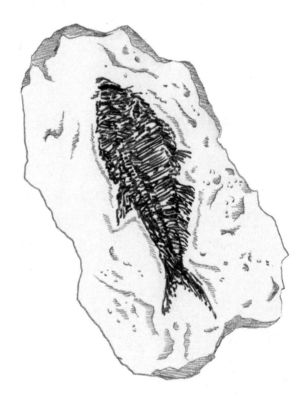

THE SOFT PARTS OF DEAD ANIMALS ROT AWAY QUICKLY. THEY DON'T STAY PRESERVED. FOSSILS USUALLY COME FROM THE HARD PARTS, LIKE A TOOTH OR BONE. A FOSSIL MAY ALSO COME FROM THE IMPRINT OF A LEAF OR FISH SCALES ON SOFT MATERIAL THAT LATER HARDENS.

THE SCIENCE OF FOSSILS IS CALLED PALEONTOLOGY. BY STUDYING FOSSILS, SCIENTISTS CAN TRACE ANIMAL LIFE BACK TO ITS EARLIEST FORMS.

ALTHOUGH PEOPLE HAD BEEN FINDING FOSSILS FOR A LONG TIME, WHEN CHARLES LIVED, SCIENTISTS DIDN'T UNDERSTAND MUCH ABOUT THEM. IN 1842 A BRITISH SCIENTIST NAMED RICHARD OWEN INVENTED THE TERM *DINOSAUR* TO DESCRIBE UNUSUAL FOSSIL BONES THAT HAD BEEN FOUND. (*DINOSAUR* MEANS "TERRIBLE LIZARD.") BUT IT WASN'T UNTIL AFTER CHARLES PUBLISHED HIS THEORY OF EVOLUTION IN 1859 THAT SCIENTISTS BEGAN TO PIECE TOGETHER THE PUZZLE OF FOSSILS.

Chapter 4
To the Galapagos

By the summer of 1834, Charles had been gone nearly three years. He'd explored many wild places. He'd visited Patagonia, Rio de Janeiro, Uruguay, and Buenos Aires. As the *Beagle* reached the southernmost tip of South America, Captain FitzRoy steered the ship carefully through the Strait of Magellan. The *Beagle* entered the Pacific Ocean safely and sailed up the western coast of South America.

CHILE

ANDES

STRAIT OF MAGELLAN

TIERRA DEL FUEGO

CAPE HORN

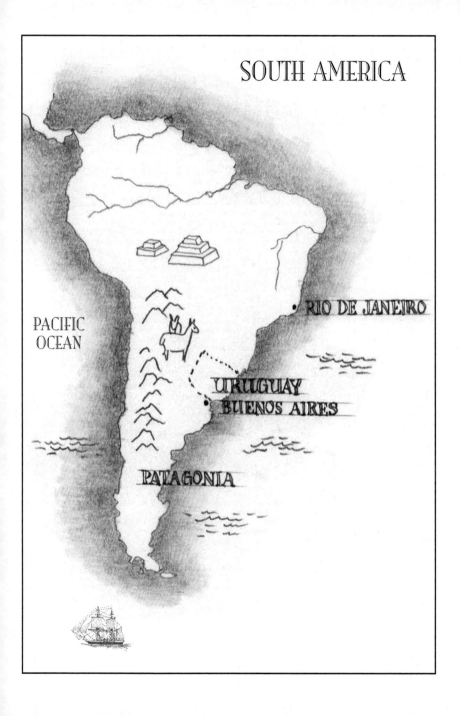

The trip had been full of adventure and danger. One time, Charles and other sailors were on Tierra del Fuego, an island near the southern tip of South America. Suddenly a huge piece of ice fell from a nearby cliff. When it hit the sea, the waves rose high. Charles thought quickly. Together, he and a sailor rushed to pull their small boat farther up the beach before it was smashed by the waves.

Captain FitzRoy stopped in the town of Valparaiso, in Chile. The *Beagle* needed repairs. Charles was glad for some time on land. He was eager to get letters from home.

Charles walked all the way to Santiago, the capital city. On the way back, he became very ill and was sick for six weeks. Up to this time, Charles had been a healthy young man. After this, he had stomach problems for the rest of his life. Charles longed to go home and almost sailed back to England on another ship. Soon after, for the first time in his life, Charles saw a volcano erupt. He also experienced an earthquake. He was so excited, he could barely sleep. For months, he'd been reading Lyell's book about the Earth, and how Earth had been formed by natural forces.

Now Charles saw this for himself. He felt the earth shake. He saw cracks open in the ground. He found bits of seashells at the top of hills. How had they gotten there? He felt sure that long ago the land had been underwater. He thought that the hills had risen up over time after volcanic eruptions.

Charles was sure Lyell was right. Natural forces like volcanoes had changed Earth in the past. And the Earth was *still* changing!

Charles climbed high into the Andes Mountains and took in everything with new, curious eyes—the shape of the rocks, the valleys below, the gravel at his feet. He tried to imagine the past, when these mountains had been pushed up from the sea by volcanic forces.

On one peak, Charles stopped to look at the glorious view. The sky was an intense blue. Wild, broken rocks lay below him. Patches of snow shone from other peaks.

More and more, Charles was seeing the world as a scientist. But the beauty of nature always moved him.

After leaving South America, the *Beagle* continued westward. The next stop was the Galapagos

Islands, off the coast of Ecuador. The *Beagle* arrived there on September 15, 1835. This was the high point for Charles. He was eager to see the amazing creatures, volcanoes, and lava fields of the Galapagos Islands.

Although few people lived on these islands, for years whaling ships had stopped to hunt and fish. Sailors were fond of capturing the giant Galapagos tortoises, which were a good source of food. They could stay alive in a ship's hold for months before being eaten.

GALAPAGOS TORTOISE

Charles was fascinated by the giant tortoises. Males can weigh up to five hundred pounds and measure five or six feet from head to tail. It seemed to Charles as if they were creatures from another planet.

Charles set off to explore. He found strange marine iguanas, which slept on warm rocks in the sun. When they got hungry, they crawled into the ocean to feed on seaweed. Charles had never seen swimming iguanas before. He wondered how these creatures, so different from any other, had come to live here.

MARINE IGUANA

THE GALAPAGOS ISLANDS

THE GALAPAGOS ISLANDS LIE IN THE PACIFIC OCEAN, SIX HUNDRED MILES WEST OF ECUADOR. THEY CONSIST OF THIRTEEN MAJOR ISLANDS AND SIX SMALLER ISLANDS. THE WORD *GALAPAGOS* MEANS "TORTOISES" IN SPANISH. MANY SPECIES ON THE ISLANDS LIVE NOWHERE ELSE ON EARTH.

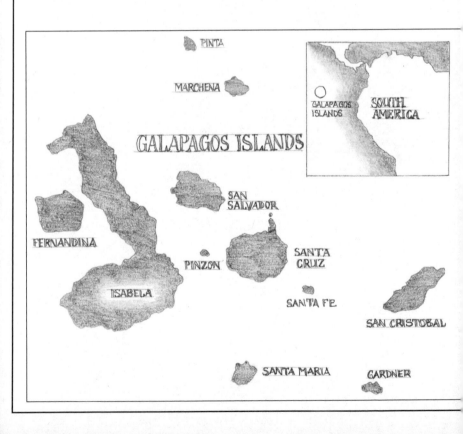

ABOUT FOURTEEN THOUSAND PEOPLE LIVE IN THE GALAPAGOS. EACH YEAR, THOUSANDS OF TOURISTS VISIT. BUT, UNLIKE CHARLES DARWIN, THEY CAN'T TAKE SPECIMENS HOME. THE GALAPAGOS NATIONAL PARK PROTECTS THE ISLANDS. CHARLES WAS THE FIRST SCIENTIST TO VISIT THE GALAPAGOS. TODAY, SCIENTISTS AT THE CHARLES DARWIN RESEARCH STATION FOLLOW IN HIS FOOTSTEPS.

Chapter 5
Secret Notebooks

From the Galapagos Islands, the *Beagle* headed west to Tahiti in the South Pacific. Then it sailed

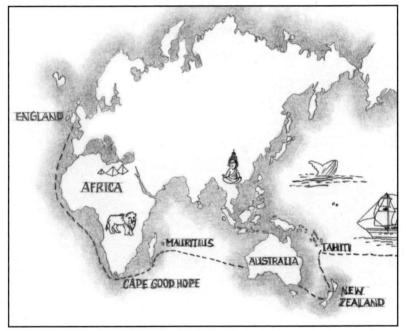

to New Zealand and Australia, and into the Indian Ocean. On the island of Mauritius, Charles had a special treat—an elephant ride! He was surprised such a large animal walked so quietly.

After a stop in South Africa, the *Beagle* sailed around the Cape of Good Hope and headed for

England. The ship docked on October 2, 1836. Three days later, Charles was back home. He was glad to see his father and the rest of his family. He'd been away for five long years.

The *Beagle* voyage had changed Charles's life. He was ready to pursue a career as a scientist. His father accepted this. There was no more talk of Charles becoming a minister.

Right away Charles set to work. Soon he was meeting famous scientists, like geologist Charles Lyell, whose book he'd read. Now the two became close friends.

Charles also began turning his *Beagle* diary into a book and spent hours sorting his collections. Charles needed the help of experts to identify

CHARLES LYELL

his finds. So he gave away many specimens to museums. The museum experts told him some of his fossils *did* belong to unknown animals. Then came even more astonishing news.

John Gould was an ornithologist, a scientist who studies birds. Gould examined the finches Charles took from the Galapagos Islands. He looked at their feathers, the shape of their beaks, the length of their bones, and other things. He wanted to know where each finch came from. But that wasn't possible because the birds hadn't been labeled that way.

Charles contacted Captain FitzRoy and other crew members who'd also collected specimens. With their help, Gould and Charles were able to identify which finches came from which islands.

Then Gould told Charles something astonishing—birds on one island were not the same species as birds from another island. They were different species! Charles was amazed. He knew that in South America there was only one finch that looked like the finches in the Galapagos Islands. Charles had assumed that the South American finch and all the Galapagos Island finches belonged to the same species. But John Gould said that was wrong.

SOUTH AMERICAN FINCH

So Charles came up with some ideas about what might have happened.

Charles thought that perhaps some finches of the South American species had gone to the Galapagos Islands long ago. Maybe a storm had blown them there. So, at first, there'd been only one species of finch on all the

GALAPAGOS FINCHES

different islands. Then, somehow, from a common ancestor, the finches on various islands changed over time, or evolved, into *different* species.

If the finches had changed, thought Charles, maybe other creatures could change, too. He hadn't forgotten the giant armadillo fossils that he'd found.

WHAT IS A SPECIES?

A *SPECIES* IS A GROUP OF SIMILAR PLANTS OR ANIMALS. SCIENTISTS USUALLY IDENTIFY A SPECIES IN TWO WAYS. FIRST, ALL MEMBERS OF THE SAME SPECIES SHARE SIMILAR CHARACTERISTICS. SECOND, INDIVIDUALS OF THE SAME SPECIES CAN *MATE* WITH ONE ANOTHER.

FOR EXAMPLE, THERE ARE MANY DIFFERENT BREEDS OF

DOGS. BUT ALL DOGS BELONG TO THE SAME SPECIES. THEY SHARE TRAITS, OR CHARACTERISTICS, FROM THEIR COMMON ANCESTORS. THEY CAN MATE AND HAVE PUPPIES. A BEAGLE AND A COLLIE WILL HAVE PUPPIES THAT ARE HALF BEAGLE, HALF COLLIE, AND *ALL DOG*.

AN EAGLE AND A SPARROW ARE DIFFERENT SPECIES. ALTHOUGH EAGLES AND SPARROWS ARE BOTH BIRDS, AND BOTH CAN FLY, THERE ARE MANY THINGS ABOUT THEM THAT ARE

DIFFERENT. THEY CAN'T MATE AND HAVE BABIES SUCCESSFULLY. THAT'S BECAUSE THEY'RE DIFFERENT SPECIES.

EVERY PLANT OR ANIMAL SPECIES HAS TWO PARTS IN ITS *SCIENTIFIC NAME*. THE FIRST PART IS THE *GENUS* (A GROUP OF SEVERAL SIMILAR SPECIES). THE SECOND PART IS THE PARTICULAR SPECIES. FOR INSTANCE, BIG CATS BELONG TO THE GROUP *PANTHERA*. A TIGER IS *PANTHERA TIGRIS*, WHILE A LION IS *PANTHERA LEO*. THEY ARE TWO DIFFERENT SPECIES.

SOME SPECIES, LIKE ZEBRAS AND GIRAFFES, ARE EASY TO TELL APART. BUT, JUST LIKE CHARLES DARWIN, EVEN TODAY SCIENTISTS SOMETIMES HAVE A HARD TIME TELLING ONE SPECIES FROM ANOTHER.

Charles couldn't help wondering if the armadillo fossils were related to the smaller, live armadillos he'd eaten.

With his own eyes, Charles had seen that changes on Earth could take place through natural forces like volcanoes. Wasn't it possible, then, that plants and animals could also change through natural force? But what was that force, and how did it work?

Charles didn't yet know. But he made up his mind to find out. And so began one of the most exciting times in Charles Darwin's life. He was on fire with questions. He poured his ideas into notebooks, which he carried everywhere. He wrote at the library, where he read book after book. He scribbled down thoughts while bumping along London streets in a carriage.

Charles also talked to people who worked with animals and plants. At the time, no one really understood *inheritance*. (That is how traits are passed from one generation to another—like brown eyes, for example.) But Charles guessed inheritance might be an important part of the puzzle.

So Charles asked his barber, who raised dogs, about breeding hounds with good hunting instincts. He also went to the zoo, looked at the

animals, and chatted with zookeepers. Charles asked questions, listened carefully, and looked closely. Yet he never told anyone *why* he was so curious.

Charles was leading a double life. To the outside world, he was a rising star in science. He was famous for his voyage on the *Beagle* and his collections. He was invited to join important groups of scientists.

But secretly, Charles was trying to solve a scientific puzzle. He didn't dare tell anyone what he was working on. Almost everyone Charles knew believed God had created the world, in just six days. The first horses and the first birds looked exactly the same at the beginning of creation as horses and birds did in Charles's time. People weren't ready to accept that the world, as they knew it, had come into being very slowly . . . and that it was still changing.

By October of 1838, Charles had a theory to explain how creatures could change. A lot of his thinking came from reading a book about human populations.

Charles realized that living creatures produce lots of offspring. Birds, for instance, have many babies. But the world isn't overrun with birds. There aren't enough resources—enough space or food—for all of them. Some birds die before they can have babies of their own. Others live longer.

They are better fit to survive and have babies of their own.

Charles knew there are many small differences, or variations, in individual members of a species. Take the finches in the Galapagos Islands. At one time, long ago, there probably had been only one species on all the islands. Even so, not all those finches looked exactly alike. For example, some finches might have been born with slightly thicker beaks than others. On an island with lots of hard seeds

THICKER BEAK

to eat, it was probably easier for the finches with thicker beaks to eat seeds. Finches with longer, narrower beaks would have had a harder time picking them up. So on this island, the long-beaked birds might not have lived as long.

Charles understood that a finch can't change the shape of its beak

NARROWER BEAK

during its lifetime. But, he figured, finches with short, thick beaks that can eat more food have a good chance of surviving long enough to have babies, or offspring, of their own. Their offspring will be part of the next *generation* of finches.

If babies in the next generation *inherit* thick beaks, they too will be better fit to survive and have offspring of their own. In other words, if the fit members are having the most babies, then each generation is more fit. The helpful trait (the thick beak) gets passed down, while unfit traits (for example, the

long narrow beak) don't get passed down as much. So each generation is more fit to survive.

In this way, over many generations, the populations of finches on the island with hard seeds are *adapting* to their environment. Over time, the population may change so much that it may eventually become a separate species. In the Galapagos Islands, over time, the finch population on an island with hard seeds to eat came to have thick, powerful beaks.

Charles guessed that this same force could explain changes in other creatures, such as the armadillos. He didn't know exactly what had happened, but he suspected that fossils could help provide important clues.

Charles understood that all creatures struggle to survive. The struggle causes populations of plants, animals, and even bacteria to change. Charles called this force *natural selection.*

Charles now had the key to part of the evolution puzzle. He had figured out something very important. But he wasn't ready to share his ideas with the world.

THE LONDON ZOO

CHARLES DARWIN LIKED TO VISIT THE LONDON
ZOO, WHERE HE COULD SEE A RHINOCEROS, AN
ORANGUTAN, AND AN ELEPHANT. THE ENGLISH HAD
LONG BEEN FASCINATED WITH EXOTIC ANIMALS.
KING HENRY I (1100-35) KEPT LIONS AND LEOPARDS
GIVEN TO HIM BY FOREIGN KINGS.
IN THE 1200S, KING HENRY III WAS GIVEN THREE
LEOPARDS, A WHITE BEAR, AND AN AFRICAN
ELEPHANT. BY 1821 THE TOWER MENAGERIE
CONTAINED OVER 280 ANIMALS. PEOPLE COULD
PAY A FEW PENNIES TO SEE THEM. THESE ANIMALS
BECAME THE CORE OF THE LONDON ZOO, WHICH
OPENED IN 1828. IN 1851, WHEN THE DARWINS
SPENT A WEEK IN LONDON, THEY TOOK
THEIR CHILDREN TO
THE ZOO. IT IS STILL A VERY
POPULAR SPOT IN LONDON.

Chapter 6
Down House

Charles was busy with his work, but he often felt lonely. Charles wanted to find someone to share his life. Of all the girls he knew, the one he liked best was his cousin, Emma Wedgwood. Emma's father was his uncle, Josiah Wedgwood, who had helped convince Charles's father to let him go around the world on the *Beagle*. Charles asked Emma to marry him. To his delight, Emma said yes. The two were married on January 29, 1839, just before his thirtieth birthday. Emma was thirty also.

That same year, Charles published his first book, *Journal of Researches*. It was based on his *Beagle* diary. And in December of 1839, the Darwins' first child, William, was born. Charles and Emma decided to move to the country to have more space for their growing family. They also hoped that Charles's stomach problems would improve by moving away from the noisy, dirty city.

The Darwins moved to a small village called Downe, sixteen miles from London. They named their home "Down House."

Charles loved exploring the fields, just like when he was a boy. He also kept writing in his

secret notebooks. By 1842 he'd begun to put his ideas about natural selection into a long paper. His first draft was thirty-five pages long. Two years later, it had grown to two hundred pages. He asked Emma to publish his paper if he died suddenly. He called the paper his "species theory."

The word *theory* has two meanings, which we can think of as "little-t theory" and "big-T theory." At this point, Charles's theory was a "little-t theory." It was a hunch that needed to be tested. In other words, Charles's "species theory" was his ideas about evolution by natural selection.

At this point, Charles's opinions were based on good evidence, such as the finches. But there wasn't enough evidence yet to call his ideas a "big-T theory." A "big-T theory" is a group of ideas, rules, or principles that explains why or how something happens.

But Charles's letter to Emma shows that he knew his ideas were very important. It also shows he was still afraid to step forward. So Charles continued to think and write in secret. He also worked on experiments, and wrote other books and scientific papers. He spent eight years studying sea creatures called barnacles. All his work helped Charles understand natural selection better.

Charles and Emma were also busy with their family. The Darwins had ten children. Three died in childhood, includ-ing Anne, their oldest

BARNACLES

HORACE
1851-1928

CHARLES WARING
1856-1858

LEONARD
1850-1943

FRANCIS
1848-1925

ELIZABETH
1847-1926

daughter, who died in 1851 when she was ten. Annie had been her father's favorite. Her death led Charles to drift away from religion.

The same year Annie died, Charles met the scientist Thomas Henry Huxley, who became a close friend. His other good friends were the geologist Charles Lyell and Joseph Hooker, a botanist. Sometimes Charles dropped hints to

GEORGE HOWARD
1845-1912

MARY ELEANOR
1842
(DIED AS AN INFANT)

ANNE ELIZABETH
1841-1851

WILLIAM ERASMUS
1839-1914

HENRIETTA EMMA
1843-1929

them about his ideas. But he wasn't ready to show his secret paper even to them.

Instead, Charles kept working to make his arguments stronger. He'd begun with scribbles in a notebook. Now he had more than two hundred thousand words! Would he ever be brave enough to publish his ideas?

FRIENDS AND SUPPORTERS OF EVOLUTION

CHARLES BELONGED TO A COMMUNITY OF SCHOLARS AND THINKERS. CHARLES'S CLOSEST SCIENTIST FRIENDS WERE:

JOSEPH HOOKER

* SIR JOSEPH DALTON HOOKER (1817-1911), A BOTANIST WHO MADE MANY EXPEDITIONS TO STUDY PLANTS.

* T. H. (THOMAS HENRY) HUXLEY (1825-1895), A BIOLOGIST KNOWN AS "DARWIN'S BULLDOG" BECAUSE HE SUPPORTED EVOLUTION SO STRONGLY. IN 1868 HE SHOWED THAT BIRDS HAD DESCENDED FROM DINOSAURS.

T. H. HUXLEY

CHARLES LYELL

* SIR CHARLES LYELL (1797-1875), A SCOTTISH GEOLOGIST WHOSE WORK HELPED EXPLAIN HOW THE EARTH WAS FORMED.

Chapter 7
The Origins of Life

In 1858, Charles received another letter that changed his life. The letter was from Alfred Russel Wallace, a naturalist living in Malaysia. With his letter, Wallace sent Charles a paper he hoped Charles might help him publish. Charles was shocked when he read Wallace's paper. Wallace had the same ideas about natural selection that he did!

Charles didn't know what to do. He had poured his heart into this work for so long, but had been too afraid to step forward. Yet if he didn't publish his ideas now, someone else would get credit for a theory he'd discovered years before.

Charles was honest, and wanted to be fair to Wallace. He told his scientist friends the truth about what he'd been working on. They came up with a plan. They would read papers by both Charles and Alfred Wallace at the same scientific meeting so both men would get credit for the discovery.

The meeting took place on July 1, 1858. Joseph Hooker first read notes on evolution that Charles had written in 1844 and 1857. Then he read Wallace's paper, written in 1858. It was clear that Charles had actually come upon the discovery first.

Alfred Wallace was not there at the meeting—he lived half the

world away. But Charles wasn't at this important meeting either. He stayed home because one of his children had become sick and died a few days before. Charles was so sad about his son's death, he could hardly think about anything else.

Although Charles didn't mind missing the meeting, he realized the time had finally come. He simply had to put all his ideas into a book. Charles worked in his study for months. He had to write down everything in longhand— there were no computers or even typewriters back then. He didn't use a desk either. He sat in a chair with a board across his knees.

By the time he finished writing in May 1859, Charles was exhausted. He went off to rest for a week at Moor Park, a place like a health spa. He tried to relax by taking walks.

Even on vacation, Charles couldn't help being curious about everything he saw. One day he came across a trail of red ants carrying cocoons. The ants were moving the cocoons from one nest to another. Along the way, some ants seemed to lose their way. Charles wondered why. He decided to watch one single ant to see what it did. Just then a tramp came along.

Charles offered him a shilling to help. The two men squatted in the road to watch ants.

A carriage drove up. The passengers stared at Charles with open mouths. They wondered about this man. He looked like a gentleman. Why was he crawling in the dirt, watching ants like a young boy? Little did they know that right before their eyes was the man whose name would soon be known throughout England . . . and then the world. For his part, Charles was just being a good scientist. All good scientists are as curious as kids!

On November 24, 1859, Charles's book was published at last. He was fifty years old. Its title was *On the Origin of Species by*

Means of Natural Selection. Today most people call it *The Origin of Species.* It is still considered one of the most important books on science ever written.

ALFRED RUSSEL WALLACE

ALFRED RUSSEL WALLACE, THE CODISCOVERER OF NATURAL SELECTION, WAS BORN IN 1823 IN WALES. ONE OF NINE CHILDREN IN A POOR FAMILY, HE COULD ONLY ATTEND SCHOOL FOR SIX YEARS. BUT LIKE CHARLES DARWIN, HE LOVED NATURE AND COLLECTING.

WALLACE DECIDED TO SEEK HIS FORTUNE BY SELLING PLANT AND ANIMAL SPECIMENS TO RICH COLLECTORS. HE WAS COLLECTING IN MALAYSIA WHEN HE WROTE HIS PAPER ABOUT NATURAL SELECTION IN 1858. WALLACE RETURNED TO ENGLAND IN 1862, WHERE HE MARRIED AND RAISED A FAMILY.

AFTER 1869, WALLACE CHANGED HIS MIND ABOUT HUMAN EVOLUTION. UNLIKE CHARLES DARWIN, WALLACE DECIDED HUMAN BEINGS HADN'T EVOLVED LIKE OTHER ANIMALS. WALLACE PUBLISHED MORE THAN TWENTY BOOKS. HE DIED IN 1913 AT AGE NINETY-ONE.

Chapter 8
Charles Darwin's Revolution

Charles Darwin felt sure there would be a revolution in science. He was right—and he was the one who started it.

The Origin of Species threw England into an uproar. Almost everyone had something to say about it. Some people attacked Charles and his ideas. Others thought his theory had to be right, even if it turned their old beliefs upside down.

"My book has stirred up the mud," Charles wrote.

In June 1860 scientists gathered for a meeting in Oxford. Charles was having stomach problems

and didn't attend. Perhaps it was just as well. The meeting turned into a huge argument about *The Origin of Species*. But as time passed, most scientists began to accept the ideas in Charles's book.

However, Charles hadn't written much about humans in *The Origin of Species*. In 1869 Alfred Russel Wallace told Charles he didn't think natural selection applied to human beings.

Charles disagreed. Once again, Wallace was the one who spurred Charles to act. Charles decided

to write what he called his "Man-book." This book, *The Descent of Man*, was published in 1871. Although the book took Charles several years to write, it was really the result of his lifetime of work. And in some ways writing the book was the most difficult task of all.

Many people still felt the only way to explain the existence of human beings was through the Bible. In the Bible, Adam and Eve are created as the first humans, looking as people do today. Charles disagreed. He said human beings were part of the animal kingdom. Humans had evolved just like other species.

Many people were outraged. Charles was sometimes drawn in cartoons as a hairy monkey swinging from a tree labeled "the tree of life." This became the symbol of evolution in people's minds.

TREE OF LIFE

In later years, Charles suffered ill health, but he kept working. He studied orchids and insect-eating plants. He also wrote his autobiography, mostly for his grandchildren. By this time, Charles was quite famous. People wrote him letters all the time. More than fourteen thousand letters to or from Charles Darwin still exist.

Charles spent his last years surrounded by his family. He published his last book in 1881. It was about earthworms. Perhaps this surprised some people. After all, Charles had written about the origins of all living creatures. Then he'd turned to something as small as worms.

But that was just like Charles Darwin. He was a true scientist, who observed the

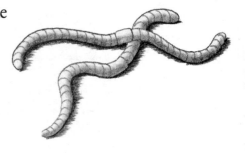

world carefully, asked questions constantly, and arrived at answers from what he saw. Filled with endless curiosity, he never stopped researching and experimenting. He knew it was possible to learn from even the smallest things in nature.

After this book, Charles slowed down. His health grew worse. He died on April 19, 1882, at age seventy-three, and was buried in Westminster

Abbey. This is where the most important people in England are laid to rest.

Today Charles Darwin's ideas are considered a cornerstone of modern science. Darwin is just as important now as he was when he lived. And scientists have been able to fill in information for much of what he could only guess at. It's amazing that Charles Darwin got so much right. After all, he didn't have the tools scientists have today. He figured out that passing traits from one generation to another was key to understanding evolution. But

WESTMINSTER ABBEY

CHARLES ROBERT DARWIN
BORN 12 FEBRUARY 1809
DIED 19 APRIL 1882

he didn't know that creatures are made up of tiny building blocks called cells. Or that DNA molecules carry instructions that control everything from the shape of our eyes and the size of our feet to the color of our hair.

Scientists now accept the process of evolution as a fact. Charles's hunch is now a "Big-T Theory." The evidence for evolution by natural selection is overwhelming. Even so, Darwin's ideas are still controversial. Some people will not accept them.

Charles himself never tired of learning, asking questions, and looking at the world with an open mind. He was never afraid to ask, how? or why? Perhaps most importantly, he had a deep love of nature.

At the end of *The Origin of Species*, his love of the natural world shines through. Charles asks his readers to think how wonderful it is just to walk along a stream, listening to birds and watching insects.

All these endlessly beautiful forms of life, Charles Darwin wrote, evolved from the simplest beginnings. Could anything be more wonderful?

CHARLES ROBERT DARWIN

February 12, 1809–

April 19, 1882

TIMELINE OF CHARLES DARWIN'S LIFE

1809 — Charles Robert Darwin is born in Shrewsbury, England, on February 12

1817 — Darwin's mother dies when he is eight

1825 — Sent to the University of Edinburgh in Scotland to study medicine

1827 — Quits medical school

1827 — Begins studying to be a minister at Cambridge University

1831 — The *Beagle* sets sail

1832 — Off the coast of Argentina, Darwin discovers fossil skeletons

1834 — In Santiago, Chile, Darwin becomes ill

1835 — The *Beagle* arrives in the Galapagos Islands, where Darwin collects birds and animals from several different islands

1836 — Returns home to England

1839 — Marries Emma Wedgwood; publishes his first book, *Journal of Researches*; first son, William, is born

1851 — Daughter Annie dies at the age of ten

1858 — Alfred Russel Wallace writes to Darwin about evolution

1859 — Darwin's *On the Origin of Species by Means of Natural Selection* is published

1871 — Darwin's *The Descent of Man* is published

1882 — Dies at the age of seventy-three and is buried in Westminster Abbey

TIMELINE OF THE WORLD

Darwin's grandfather publishes one of the first theories on evolution — **1794**

The first successful journey of a steamboat, the *Clermont*, in New York — **1807**

Webster's Dictionary is published — **1806**

Napoleon Bonaparte is exiled and Louis XVIII becomes King of France — **1814**

Beethoven writes *Symphony No. 9* — **1823**

Regent's Park Zoo opens in London — **1828**

Daguerreotype photography is presented in Paris — **1839**

British scientist Richard Owen invents the term "dinosaur" — **1842**

The British Factory Act limits the working day for women and children to ten hours — **1847**

Charles Dickens publishes *David Copperfield* — **1850**

Neanderthal skull found near Düsseldorf, Germany — **1856**

Abraham Lincoln is elected president of the United States — **1860**

Jean Bernard Léon Foucault measures the speed of light — **1862**

Civil War ends — **1865**

The skeleton of Cro-magnon man, the first Homo sapiens in Europe, is found in France — **1868**

The United States turns one hundred; Alexander Graham Bell invents the telephone — **1876**

BIBLIOGRAPHY

Barlow, Nora, ed. **The Autobiography of Charles Darwin 1809–1882.** W. W. Norton & Company, New York, 1958.

Browne, Janet. **Charles Darwin: Voyaging.** Alfred A. Knopf, New York, 1995.

Browne, Janet. **Charles Darwin: The Power of Place.** Alfred A. Knopf, New York, 2002.

Darwin, Charles. **The Origin of Species.** 1859.

Darwin, Charles. **The Descent of Man.** 1871.

Heller, Ruth. **Galapagos Means Tortoises.** Gibbs Smith Publishers, Salt Lake City, Utah, 2003.

Keynes, R. D., ed. **Charles Darwin's Beagle Diary.** Cambridge University Press, Cambridge, U.K., 1988.

Mayr, Ernst. **What Evolution Is.** Basic Books, New York, 2001.

Sis, Peter. **The Tree of Life: Charles Darwin.** Farrar, Straus and Giroux, New York, 2003.

For Further Information

For more information about the Galapagos Islands and the Charles Darwin Research Station, visit www.darwinfoundation.org

To learn more about Peter and Rosemary Grant's research on Darwin finches, visit www.pbs.org/wgbh/evolution/library